The Blue Cow

and her fantastic exploits

Publisher's Note

Since 1886, FREEDOM PRESS have been publishing anarchist propaganda. As well as the forthightly journal *Freedom* and the 96-page quarterly review *The Raven*, there are some 70 Freedom Press titles, books and pamphlets in print. We are also the distributors for a number of small publishers. Please send for our complete catalogue.

As mentioned in the foreword to *The Blue Cow*, this title is by the same artist who produced *The March to Death* (see page 67) and not a typical FREEDOM PRESS title. Yet in our hard, cynical world we feel sure that *The Blue Cow* will bring a big smile to all generations for her antics and, to her creator, appreciation for a great artist of the simple line.

FREEDOM PRESS
84b Whitechapel High Street
London E1 7QX

The Blue Cow

and her fantastic exploits

by John Olday

Freedom Press 1996

First published 1996
by Freedom Press
84b Whitechapel High Street
London E1 7QX

© Freedom Press

ISBN 0 900384 86 7

printed in Great Britain by Aldgate Press,
Unit 5, Gunthorpe Street Workshops, Gunthorpe Street, London, E1

Foreword

When I first met John (Jo) Olday (1905-1977) at Freedom Press in early 1942 he was in uniform and in the Pioneer Corps. As I have written elsewhere, " I do know from personal involvement that he was 'on the run' for almost two years before being picked up in December 1944". During that period 'on the run' he produced many political cartoons for *War Commentary* and the volume *March to Death* (1943) which Freedom Press have just reprinted.*

He gave this collection of drawings and text of *The Blue Cow* to Marie Louise Berneri, who had looked after his daily material needs while he was 'on the run', to do with them as she wished. It was a time when paper was rationed, and it was felt that *The Blue Cow* was not material for Freedom Press. Marie Louise nevertheless tried to find commercial publishers which would provide funds for Jo when he came out of detention. She produced a synopsis and a French translation, in the hope that her French contacts could find a publisher after the war. Marie Louise died in 1949.

I found *The Blue Cow* again in 1995, while looking for something else in my four-tier filing cabinet. While I still would not suggest that it is a Freedom Press title, it is a volume for all anarchist parents and their children to enjoy. The printing costs have been paid for by a Freedom Press well-wisher who wants the proceeds from sales to be put to the Freedom Press overheads solidarity fund.

So, enjoy *The Blue Cow* as I have (though I have not yet come across a blue liquid that raises my spirits) and at the same time know that you are contributing to a good cause.

Vernon Richards
January 1996

*84pp ISBN 0 900 384 80 8 £3.00 (see page 67)

Author's Introduction

Now don't say: whoever heard of a blue cow? It's true you won't find her in the Zoo. Farmers don't know anything about her and she is not mentioned in the books by Darwin. But that doesn't prove that there are no blue cows.

Of course, if you ask one of those people who know an answer to everything, they too will say "Blue cow? There are no blue cows!"

But you ask an artist or a poet – if you happen to know any – or ask somebody who is called a dreamer by his friends, and he'll tell you different.
Perhaps you are a dreamer yourself. You are? In that case I can speak to you as one dreamer to another.

Ever hear of "blue hours"? Blue hours are dreamers' best hours. Not those sunny hours when one dreams in the blue sky. No, I mean the twilight, the fireside hours. When the outside world begins to quieten down, when the crickets chirp in the fields, when the dawn comes and the shadows fall. Those are the blue hours.

You look up at the ceiling and it is as if you are looking at a sky of floating clouds. Your mind begins to wander from the present to the past, from the past into the future. And then...your room seems to be filled with blue mist and shadows, developing into forms. You watch them coming into life and disappearing. You see figures, people, in old-fashioned dresses. You see Indians, pirates, soldiers, princes, magicians, golden castles and silver mountains, flying witches and dragons. You even hear them.

Sometime those worlds are more real than real life. The colours are brighter and more beautiful than anything you have ever seen before. You could not copy them, even if you were the greatest painter on earth. But most times there seems to be a veil between you and your dreamland. What you see lives and moves behind a transparent curtain of thin bluish glass a wall of blue mist. That's why I call those twilight hours, "blue hours".

Never mind what people who never dream may say. Those blue hours are next door to the world's first beginning. They are the spring of all tales, poems, songs and master-pieces. There would not be a world without blue hours, and no future could come without them.

The blue hour is the mother of all inspirations, all grand thoughts. Whatever man has created, built up, made real – it was unreal before, a dream in one of those quiet blue hours.

But not only deep and wonderful thoughts, stories, poems, melodies, pictures and inventions are born in blue hours. The favourite child of the blue hours is: humour. I bet you have sometimes dreamt in one of your blue hours of something extremely funny and silly. So silly that it made you burst with laughter.

You have? And did it also happen that when you wanted to tell your friends what made you laugh, you just couldn't make them see it the way you saw it? My blue cow used to appear again and again in my blue hours. She has given me a lot of fun. So I decided to draw and write down some of her adventures and show them to my friends. And "my" blue cow became "our" blue cow.

If she gives you as much fun as she gave me, she will most likely come to visit you as well in your own blue hours. And perhaps one day you will be able to tell us a few new funny stories of – **Our Blue Cow!**

John Olday
London, 1945

Chapter One

"Artists without dreams are like birds without wings!"

That's what our artist told me. He ought to know because he is a great artist but, as he himself admits, he is a far greater dreamer.

He used to dream about landscapes, still-life and so on, until one day the blue cow appeared in one of his dreams. When he saw her first he was quite surprised.

"Well," he said. "You're the most extraordinary cow I've ever seen!" The blue cow was greatly flattered. Of course, she hardly knew how strange it was to be a blue cow. She knew nothing at all, because she had just been born and thought that she and the artist and the room in which she found herself were the only things in the world.

The artist laughed at her being so simple. (As you know, when one dreams, one can read the thoughts of others).

"Well, " he said. "This being your first birthday, somebody ought to take the place of your good fairy and present you with a special gift. Is there anything you would particularly like?"

The blue cow could not think of anything.

"Let's see," said the artist. "We can live without many things which people believe they can't do without. But there is one thing no-one can really do without. I therefore hereby present to you your first birthday present, a brand-new self-consciousness".

The blue cow, rather dumbfounded, took the invisible present. Not knowing what exactly she had to do with it, she ate it.

It was just the right amount, not too little and not too much. It tasted neither sweet nor sour. But as soon as she had swallowed it she felt altogether different, and looked at the artist as if she wanted some more. "Better not," he said. "Too much is always unwelcome. How do you feel now?"

The blue cow felt odd. She did not know what she wanted, but she wanted it very badly!

"You haven't digested your self-consciousness yet," explained the artist. "But never mind – you'll be all right. You know you're the best thing I've ever dreamed up. If I had the choice between you and the golden cow, I would without hesitation choose you."

"Who's the golden cow?" asked the blue cow.

So the artist had to tell her the story of the golden cow.

Put yourself in the position of the blue cow!

Up till now she had not the slightest idea of anything else existing except herself, the artist and his room. Now she learned that there were millions of other human beings, all of whom she imagined to look like her artist. And there were deserts, mountains, clouds, sun and sky, earth and sea, and millions and millions of animals.

She tried hard to sort things out, but the artist, still talking, gave her no time.

"You see," he said. "The people were worshipping the golden cow, and some still do it nowadays. I can tell you that many would give almost anything to have a golden cow. But still, you're made out of something more rare than gold, something one cannot buy for all the gold in the world. If I wanted to, I could make a picture of you as I usually do with my dreams. But this time I shall keep you as you are, all for myself. You will not be for sale, not at any price. That ought to make you feel proud!"

But the blue cow only felt confused. She was still trying to picture all the strange things the artist had told her. And if I were to draw them for you, the way she imagined them, it would fill a book and would make you roar with laughter.

"Now then," said the artist. "You don't look very happy. You look nearly as stupid as one of those ordinary, real cows."

The blue cow nearly fainted. What! Wasn't she real?

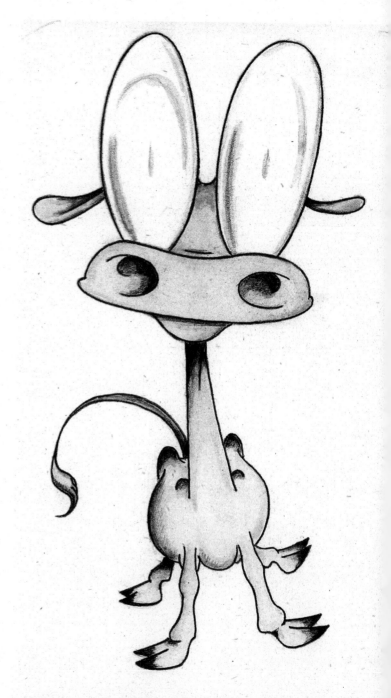

"Well," said the artist. "You are and you're not. You are my dream-cow, my imagination. But that's the best thing you could ever be. You ought to congratulate yourself, you know. Anybody else but me would easily have made a bad job of you. Even nature makes mistakes. She sometimes creates cows with two heads, three tails, four horns and a dozen legs. Just think, if I had made you that way! Or just picture yourself in a different, ordinary condition. And supposing I'd given you eyes as big as mirrors or searchlights. You would frighten people out of their wits. Another artist would have made you totally different. Would you, for instance, like to be a cubistic cow, made out of squares and quadrangles? Or would you fancy yourself being formed out of circles and ellipses? Of course you wouldn't!

"You're not only as good as any real cow, you're even better. Why, you don't have to eat and drink to keep yourself alive. You don't even have to pull a plough or cart. You need do nothing at all if you don't wish to, and what puts you above all real beings is that whatever you want to do you *can* do, for nothing is impossible for a dream-cow. Now, what do you say?"

The blue cow couldn't say anything, because the idea simply took her breath away.

14

Day after day, whenever the artist began to dream, the blue cow came to visit him. He told her stories about the world, about himself. I wish I could tell you what they saw when they both went through his dream-land. They were the most wonderful, the most beautiful, the strangest and most exciting adventures a cow ever had.

But there were times when the world didn't permit him to dream, when he had to be busy rushing about his everyday business. And then the blue cow felt very lonely and lost. When she told her artist about it, he said: "Why don't you stroll about on your own? You can always come back when I need you, and you'll have a lot to tell me about all your experiences."

So she decided that whenever she felt lonely she would go out on her own.

Chapter Two

The blue cow's first adventures were upwards into the sky. Jumping from cloud to cloud she kept on climbing up and up and up. After some time she got rather tired and disappointed. Heaven, of which she expected so much, seemed to be nothing but an endless, empty nothing. So she just sat down on a cloud and let it drift along with her on it.

Looking up she suddenly sighted a little silver spot high up above. It grew bigger and bigger until it began to assume some sort of shape. When she drifted nearer still she discovered that it was a horse. A horse with wings.

"Hallo!" she said to the horse with wings.

"By Zeus!" replied the horse, who was Pegasus, the horse of poets. "In this Olympic sphere we greet one another in Latin!"

"Sorry," said the blue cow. "I don't know Latin."

"Scandal!" snorted Pegasus. "What are we coming to! Profane, prosaic cows in the sphere of poets! Haven't they any poets to send up?" He looked disdainfully down at the earth.

"I don't know," stammered the blue cow.

"In my time," said Pegasus, "The whole cosmos, every living creature, knew of the great living poets. What are we coming to! And, by the way, who are you?"

"I'm the blue cow," said the blue cow.

"You haven't even got wings," said Pegasus.

"I don't need wings," said the blue cow, "Because I'm an extraordinary cow."

Actually, Pegasus, if the truth were known, was not anything as haughty as he appeared to be. He was only bad-tempered. Because it was such a long time since the last mortal had come up to the sphere of immortal poetry.

"Well," he asked. "What do you want up here?"

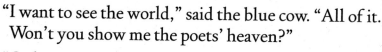

"I want to see the world," said the blue cow. "All of it. Won't you show me the poets' heaven?"

"Only poets can enter the poets' heaven," said Pegasus.

"Well, that's that," said the blue cow. "What can't be, can't be."

"I'm sorry," said Pegasus. "All I can let you see is the land of imagination"

"Is it as wonderful as dream-land?" asked the blue cow.

"Almost!" said Pegasus. "In the land of imagination you'll find many interesting things. You see, the heaven of the great poets is the highest, but just underneath is the heaven of fairy-tales. There you'll find everything that has been imagined by the people up till now. Dreamland, which is on the other side of darkness and light, holds many still undiscovered things. It is the paradise of poets, lovers, children and fools, but it has a lower world, which is hell for the wicked."

To make her see the land of imagination, Pegasus brushed his tail three times over her eyes, and when she looked round again the whole sky was filled with fairies, gnomes, goblins, giants, angels, ghosts and dragons, and from behind an enormous white bank of clouds came rays of heavenly light.

"That's grand," said the blue cow, pointing at the place from which the flood of light was coming. "I want to go to Heaven!"

"Who doesn't," said Pegasus. "But it isn't as easy as you think. First of all, what Heaven do you want to go to? Next, what Heaven are you entitled to?"

Seeing the surprise of the blue cow, he said: "Well, you see, there are many heavens. There are as many heavens as there are cultures and religions. You need a ticket for each one. If you want to enter the poets' heaven, you've got to present the golden wreath of fame, the light of genius. No-one can enter the Catholic heaven without having had the sacraments, and so on. Before you can enter any of them you must first present a proper testimonial."

"Well," said the blue cow, "If I can't get into one of them, I do wish I had one of those glorious haloes!"

"Ridiculous," said Pegasus. "A cow with a halo?"

"Why not?" said the blue cow. "Haven't you got wings like one of those angels?"

"That's different," Pegasus said, like all people say when they know no better answer. "Haloes are only for saints and holy people. Why, even the sacred animals have no halo!"

"Sacred animals!" the blue cow cried. "Please, do show me the sacred animals."

Pegasus told her to get hold of her own tail, to close her eyes, and then to keep on turning in a circle until she was completely dizzy. Having reached that state she was allowed to open her eyes, and looking up, she could see right into the heaven of the holy animals. There she saw white elephants, monkeys and cats and bulls.

"Not very exciting," she said. "They look terribly bored."

"So they are," Pegasus confirmed. "That's because they don't get as much incense and sacrifices as in the old days. Nowadays only Hindoos still have their sacred animals. But in the old days animals were worshipped all over the world by many nations."

"I see," said the blue cow, rather dejectedly.

"Don't be sad," Pegasus said. "I've got something very nice to show you." Then before she realised what was happening, she found herself in the paradise of the ordinary animals.

20

It was a most delightful place. Animals of all kinds living without fear of one another, playing, dancing in joy and happiness.

Each one had had his wishes granted. You could see elephants and pigs with wings, fish swimming through the air, a tree that did not have to stand for ever on one spot but was able to move about and walk. There were mushrooms dancing about, and flowers flying, like butterflies, from place to place.

It was such a charming sight that the blue cow forgot her disappointment. "This really is heaven!" she said.

When they had left the happy land of peace and fulfilled wishes, Pegasus bade farewell to the blue cow and wished her all the best on her journey. And the blue cow gave him a big kiss as a reward for all he had shown her, clambered onto a passing cloud, and waved to him with her tail until he was lost from her sight.

She noticed that it was beginning to get dark. Here and there a star began to shine. She headed towards a bigger cloud, on which she wanted to sail back in comfort, and on reaching it saw the moon hiding behind. And on the moon she saw a very, very sleepy and unhappy looking man.

"My word," she said. "You do look unhappy. Whatever is the matter?"

"I'm so tired of life," yawned the man-in-the-moon. "So terribly tired. Aren't you?"

"No," said the blue cow. "Life is quite exciting."

"Not for me," said the man-in-the-moon. "If you had to live my life, you wouldn't find it worthwhile either. Look at me. For thousands and thousands of years I've been lonely – imprisoned in this magic ball. For thousands and thousand of years, I have been travelling in a big circle round and round. Always the same route, always seeing the same stars. It's awful – there's no other word for it – it's simply awful." The tears were running down his cheeks and dropping like pearls into the darkness.

"You see," he sobbed, pointing at those falling, disappearing tears. "Every night I have to cry. Cry and cry and cry and cry. The earth is covered with my tears which the humans call dew. Nobody ever imagines those drops could be tears. It's awful, it's simply awful!"

"Poor man," said the blue cow, nearly moved to tears herself. "How you must suffer!"

"That's not all," the man-in-the-moon cried. "Sometimes I can't cry. The spring seems to be dried and when no more tears come, a dreadful thing happens – again and again. The black magic power of darkness which now surrounds me begins to press me, and pound me, and squeezes more tears out of me. "

At that moment the blue cow witnessed those dreadful happenings for herself, saw how the poor man-in-the-moon got squeezed and squeezed and squeezed, until he was squeezed into the shape of a thin sickle. All the time he was crying, "It's awful, it's really too awful!" and the tears were flowing from his eyes in streams.

"Oh," said the blue cow, deeply moved. "This is really awful – too awful for words."

24

It took some time for the man-in-the-moon to regain his full shape and by then he was completely exhausted.

"What you need is a holiday," said the blue cow. "Why don't you come with me for a nice long walk?"

"I wish I could," replied the man-in-the-moon. "But I can't get out of this ball. It's awful – it's ... "

"Never mind," said the blue cow, interrupting him. "I'll carry you and your round prison." So she did. She took him in his transparent ball on her back, and off they went.

The sky was cloudless. So the blue cow had to use the stars, stepping from one to the next, very carefully and slowly. Suddenly they were surprised by a challenging voice:

"Who goes there?"

Looking up they saw a woman with four children, whose large surprised eyes were nearly as bright and big as the stars. And then the woman added:

"Whatever are you two doing?"

"We're out for a ride!" said the blue cow. "The man in-the-moon needs a rest!"

"My, my," said the woman, shaking her head. "And who's taking his place?"

"They'll have to do without him," said the blue cow.

You should have heard what the woman had to say. Did she tell them off! Leaving the world without dew and in the dark!

"Look at you," she said to the man-in-the-moon. "You're already losing your brightness!" And then, seeing that the blue cow was standing on stars, she got really bad-tempered and cried, "Well, blow me down!" (And that is a very dangerous thing to say up there in the sky). "Will you get off those stars, you big monster? Look at those poor little things. You've bent them out of shape, you've dirtied them, you...you..."

"Who's she?" whispered the blue cow to the man-in-the-moon.

"The charwoman of heaven," he explained. "She has to keep things clean up here. The skylarks and cloud-monsters always carry earthdust on their feet and trample and stamp it all over the blue sky-meadow. Besides keeping the sky dust-free, she also has to polish the stars and her children are engaged polishing the haloes of the angels. It's quite a job, you know." .

"Yes," interrupted the woman. "And when one has things just so, you come along and spoil everything and make twice as much work!"

"I'm terribly sorry," said the blue cow. "I had no idea." And she promised to dust and polish the stars and bend them back into shape, as soon as she could get a lift on a sailing cloud.

The woman disappeared as suddenly as she had appeared.

"You see," the man-in-the-moon said. "Nobody on earth knows anything of the charwoman of the sky. They can't see her in the dark. If it wasn't for her, the stars would go blind, the sky black, even during daytime."

"She ought to wear a big, bright medal," the blue cow sighed, "Or a big, big halo. Then maybe people would see her and pay homage to her."

The charwoman of the sky went to see the winds, who lived in a nearby cloud village.

Lovely, longhaired Spring winds; tall, peace-loving evening winds; heavy Summer-day winds. Little baby winds and boyish breezes, the spinster cold draughts as well as the big fat pressures, the wild whirlwind, the thunderstorms and hurricanes. She told them that the man-in-the-moon had left his job and the winds promised to get things back to normal right away.

So they went to look for the blue cow and when they found her they all blew together with all their strength in order to blow the moon back to his proper place. They blew so hard that a big star got unstuck and fell, drawing a long trail of glittering light through the darkness. It came screaming at the blue cow, who had to jump to one side. And as she jumped the man-in-the-moon was jolted, lost his balance and fell from her back. And along came the winds and carried him away.

Chapter Three

For her next journey the blue cow wanted to meet people, and see what the earth looked like. So first of all she made a trip round the globe on a sailing cloud, enjoying her view of the earth, with its towns and villages, fields and hills, mountains, seas and forests . Then she decided to visit a little town in a small but beautiful hilly country. She came walking over the hills in the dead of night, and when she reached the little town there were no more lights and eveybody seemed to be asleep.

Carefully feeling her way over the roofs of the houses, she passed a church and there on top of the tower sat a silver cock, who was startled out of his wits by the strange sight of an enomous blue cow walking over the roofs. "Good evening," said the blue cow to the silver cock. But the poor cock nearly fell from his stand, and his eyes nearly popped out of his head. "Please don't be frightened," begged the blue cow. "D-didn't you c-c-come f-from u-up there?" stuttered the silver cock.

For your information, dear reader, the cock was dumb, but in the same way as speaking people can lose their voices through a great shock, the cock, who had no voice, began to talk under the shock! The blue cow nodded in a friendly way. And the silver cock gave a great sigh of relief. Then, all of a sudden, he realised that he had spoken, and he got so excited that he nearly lost his newly-found gift of speaking. "D-didn't I sp-speak?" he asked, excitedly.

"Why, yes," said the blue cow. The silver cock was overwhelmed.

"A miracle," he whispered, listening to his own whispering, doubtful and fearful lest it should vanish as suddenly as it had appeared. He whispered again and again, to make sure he wasn't dreaming, each time a bit louder, until there could no longer be the slightest doubt.

Then he got extremely talkative, as if he had to make up for his long years of silence. "I am no longer dumb," he babbled hurriedly. "I can talk! And if I can talk, I can also crow! It's wonderful, it's ... Oh, you don't know what it means. You see, there's a real cock living down there in the parson's house. The most conceited, arrogant cock in the whole wide world. How he looks, sneers and jeers at me, that supercilious bird. Because I'm silver, because I have no real feathers, no harem, and had no voice. His father did the same and before him his grandfather. They were only jealous because they never could reach up to me, while I could look down on them. But now – now – I shall be able to crow, I shall crow him out of his sleep – I ..."

"Please don't," said the blue cow. "Not just now. You'll set the whole town in an uproar. Wait till the morning."

"Very well," said the silver cock, swallowing his eagerness. "But when the morning comes, I'll crow so loudly that they'll think the day of judgement has arrived."

"A pity you can't show me around," said the blue cow.

"Why not?" asked the silver cock. "I'm sick of sitting here anyhow. Just lift me off and place me on your back. But I must get back in time to crow, that's all."

So the blue cow took the silver cock off its perch, and the silver cock led the blue cow around the town, and showed her everything worth seeing.

When they came to the centre of the town they heard music coming from the market-place and looking over the roofs from behind the tower, they saw a group of townspeople serenading one of the sleeping town beauties.

It was the first time the blue cow had ever heard music and she was really moved by it.

The silver cock was less impressed. His eyes were fixed eastwards, in order not to miss the very first sign of daybreak.

The blue cow, carried away by her emotions, forgot herself completely and began to sing. At the same moment the silver cock had seen the first sign of daybreak and started crowing – Cock-a-doodle-doo!

The musicians were horror-stricken. They thought there had been an earthquake or something equally terrible. And when they saw the singing blue cow, and on her back the crowing silver cock, panic overtook them and they ran for their lives, leaving behind their poor conductor, who had fainted, being over-sensitive as musicians generally are.

The silver cock, crowing himself to triumph, went out of control, overdid his strength and burst into a hundred little silver pieces, which rained down onto the streets like small glittering stars.

The townspeople fell out of their beds and thought that the end of the world had come. Their houses were shaking, their window-panes were cracked, and splintered plates fell from the kitchen-dressers. Doors sprang open, and even after the cow had stopped, her voice still sounded in the air like the roar of a hundred guns.

In every house the people were hiding under their creaking beds, even the bravest not daring to show their faces. Only a few daring nosey young scamps had a look out of the windows . But when they saw the blue cow they flew back screaming and disappeared hastily under their mothers' aprons.

The blue cow, having no idea what horror she had caused, was rather surprised that nobody came out to join in her singing. She looked around and saw, some distance away, a lot of people gathering in the fields. They were moving about like ants.

How was she to know that the horrified musicians had warned the Army? There they came, marching up in battle order, taking positions to fight and destroy the blue monster that had invaded their town.

The blue cow, in all her innocence and inexperience, thought they were coming to give her a welcome and play with her.

Even when they fired the first red-hot cannon balls at her, she didn't realise that it meant war, but thought they wanted to play ball with her.

So she caught the cannon balls, had great fun juggling with them for a while, and then, when the soldiers fired more, threw them back, using her feet and tail and horns. She was highly delighted because she never missed one, and when those she threw back landed on the other side, and exploded with a big bang, she thought that was all part of the game.

Well – the battle didn't last long. No army can fight against an unkillable, super-human creature. The Army general, seated at his table at headquarters, was already wondering what had happened, when his exhausted trumpeter brought him the news that the whole army was in a full disorderly retreat.

Up jumped the general from his map-covered table, took his sword and said, "If they all quit – I shall fight on alone!" And with the battle-cry, "No surrender!" he marched off towards the battlefield.

When the shaking town councillors saw him going to fight all alone, they blocked his way and begged him not to go. But he, being not only a general but also a hero, snapped back, "No!" His answer rang like a gunshot.

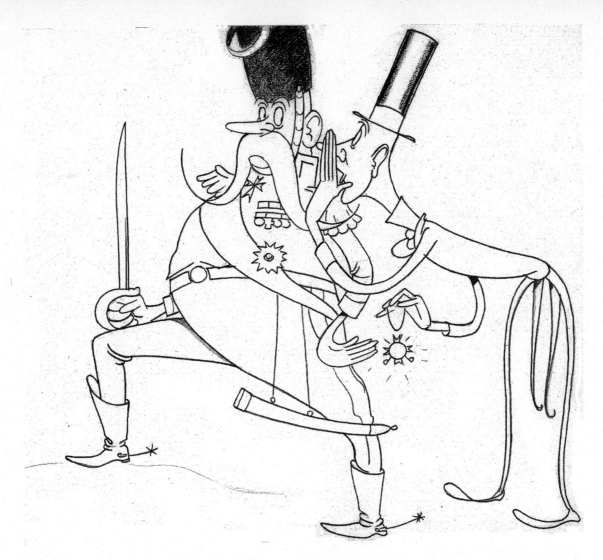

But then came the Mayor of the town, who was a very clever diplomat. You could see how clever and important he was, by the way he whispered into the general's ear.

He said that the general could render a greater service to the town by persuading the blue cow to become their ally. No enemy would ever dare to attack them with such an ally. And if the general succeeded in his mission, the town would award him the highest decoration it had, and on top of this, two special orderlies he had always wanted, to carry the ends of his long, heavy moustaches.

You may find a general who will face certain death without flicking an eyelid, but you won't find a single general who could resist such a tempting offer.

So the general went forward with a white flag, escorted by the elders, to negotiate with the blue cow, and the blue cow when asked, said, "Yes, she would be their ally."

46

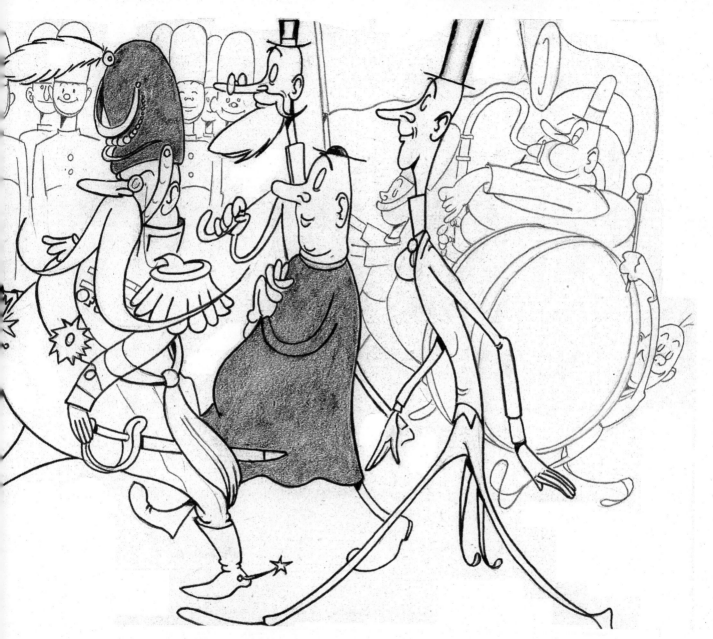

And so the general got his decoration and was made marshal (the orderlies he could not have because of the shortage of new recruits). The blue cow got a golden wreath of victory, the town a new blue flag, and everybody was satisfied.

Chapter Four

Soon after the blue cow had visited the sky and the human beings, she felt that she would like to see some of the real animals the artist had told her about.

She left the people of the town after promising she would return whenever they needed her.

Again she travelled on a sailing cloud, passing over many beautiful places, until she saw a herd of real cows, led by a big, strong, handsome bull, grazing on a hillside.

So down she went.

This time she reduced her size, in order not to frighten anybody.

The big, strong, handsome bull was nevertheless speechless, as were the cows, when suddenly out of the blue sky a blue cow appeared in front of them.

"Hallo," said the blue cow and tried to look as normal and ordinary as possible. Having had no practice in speaking with real cows and bulls she, of course, behaved in a most uncowish way, causing alarm among the animals present.

The big, strong, handsome bull stared and stared. The cows even stopped chewing the cud and that shows you how perplexed they were.

The blue cow gave the big, strong, handsome bull her very best smile and wink.

But there they stood, the big, strong, handsome bull and the speckled cows, motionless, not even moving their tails.

So the blue cow, eager to show herself to better advantage, and to create an impression on the big strong handsome bull, began to paint. Yes – I said paint. Using the tip of her tail as a painting brush she painted the portrait of the big, strong, handsome bull on the nearby wall. But did the cows appreciate it? They didn't! I doubt very much if those cows could be normal cows – you sometimes see them gathered round a painter who has planted his easel in the middle of a meadow. Anyhow, the big, strong, handsome bull, recognising himself in the

portrait, was flattered. And the blue cow, encouraged, but very much embarrassed at being surrounded by those stupid, glaring cows, thought of talking to the big, strong, handsome bull in the special language of art (which the cows didn't seem to understand) by dancing.

And so she danced. And the big, strong, handsome bull began to beat the rhythm, first with his hoofs and tail, and then – with his heart.

Having got so far the blue cow made a harp out of the bull's horns, and played tunes on it, sang sweet songs of Spring, moonlight and – of love .

Never had the big, strong, handsome bull heard anything so sweet and wonderful. Never had his heart felt more captivated. He forgot all the other cows and had eyes and ears only for her, the one and only blue cow. And as for the blue cow, her gaze was directed on him, the one and only big, strong, handsome bull.

They both felt as if they were far, far away from those disgusted cows all around them, as if they were far, far away on some lonely island.

The cows were furious with this carrying-on. They got together and discussed the matter and they were all of one opinion: that the blue cow was – well, I had better not repeat what these jealous cows did say! And when they had just reached the end of their gossiping and tittle-tattle, the blue cow and the big, strong, handsome bull came ambling by.

So one of the cows, the former favourite of the bull, said as loud as she could: "A blue cow is all very well, but – can she produce milk?"

The blue cow and the big, strong, handsome bull were stumped by that remark! The blue cow looked at the big, strong, handsome bull and he at her. No-one but the blue cow could have behaved in such a dignified way in such an awkward situation. She went behind a tree. And the big, strong, handsome bull acted as her escort. And there she tried and tried and tried. And the big, strong, handsome bull himself was as worried as she was, and beads of perspiration poured down his face. And all the time she was behind the tree the other cows were watching and waiting in the distance.

But then – the bull heard something. He listened again to make quite sure. Yes, she was coming from behind the tree carrying a bucket. And it was full of milk! He was so overjoyed he nearly shouted "Hooray!"

You should have seen the faces of the other cows! And you should have seen how proud the big strong, handsome bull was as he marched by the side of the blue cow, carrying the milk-bucket to the farmer who was with his wife and the farm-lad. And then you should have seen their puzzled faces!

They looked in turn at the blue cow, at the big, strong, handsome bull, at the milk-bucket, at the other cows, at each other, and once more at the blue cow. They just couldn't make head or tail of it!

Then they looked at the milk more closely – would you believe it, the milk was blue! Sky-blue, in fact, as blue as the blue cow!

Blue milk! The cows roared with laughter. A cock sitting on top of a dung-heap crowed as loud as he could, "Blue milk!" The cocks of the neighbourhood at once crowed back questioning, "Blue milk?" The whole farm was in an uproar. The hens, the geese, the ducks, running all over the place, quacking, cackling, clucking, spitefully and maliciously telling everyone who crossed their path, "Blue milk – blue milk". "Blue milk", grunted the pigs, laughed the pigeons, neighed the horses, barked the dog and miaowed the cat!

It was terrible!

The only ones not laughing were the farmer, his wife and the boy. They were quite angry about the uproar!

And there stood the poor blue cow, a picture of misery and dejection, and the big, strong, handsome bull, as puzzled and worried as he could be.

It was a heartbreaking sight.

The blue cow gave one more sad glance at the big, stro,ng handsome bull and then turned and went away, and went sadly, her head bent, her tail hanging limply.

She had not gone far when she heard the sound of galloping hoofs. Turning around she saw the big, strong, handsome bull rushing towards her, and when he reached her, all out of breath, and with a desperate look in his eye, he said, "Blue milk or white milk – you're my girl cow!"

The blue cow felt a lump in her throat and tears in her eyes. She was so moved she could not even whisper. All she could do was to move close beside her big, strong, handsome bull, rest her chin on his back, and close her eyes in deep, deep joy.

There they stood. The blue cow and the big, strong, handsome bull. He slung his tail round her neck; united they were, facing a cold and hostile world – two great and true lovers.

The other cows, having seen the big, strong, handsome bull deserting them, went out of their minds. They called a great protest meeting of all the farm animals. Everyone was talking at the same time, each trying to shout down everybody else. The noise was terrific, until one of the cows demanded silence, and speaking in the name of all the cows, said that something ought to be done. Everyone agreed.

So they all decided in favour of going on strike. They would give no more milk or wool and lay no more eggs. They would fast and get so skinny that the farmer would be forced to drive the blue cow away and make the big, strong, handsome bull come back, to his cows.

But in the meantime something else had happened.

The farmer had dipped his fingers into the blue milk, and found that it had rather a pleasant taste. So the farmer's wife dipped a finger in too and tasted and so did the farmer's boy.

And they licked their lips, and smacked their lips, and they looked at each other in amazement and delight, and they took a little sip, then a mouthful and finally a whole glassful and they smiled and grinned and felt strangely merry and happy and then – then they began to dance!

The farmer's wife jumped and jigged and giggled. The farmer forgot his lumbago and jumped like a young lamb, and the boy threw his arms and legs up into the air and shouted – Whoopee!

They danced and sang, and sang and danced. They forgot about their farm, their work, their striking animals, all their everyday worries and troubles, and felt as if they could embrace and kiss the whole world.

The news of these strange happenings spread like wildfire. People were meeting in the street of the next village, and asking each other, "Have you heard? Have you heard?" The Mayor came and asked: "What's that – what's that?" And when told he muttered, "We must look into this!" So they all went to see the farmer, his wife and the boy.

When the mayor and his party arrived and saw the farmer, his wife and the boy as if without a care in the world, they were most disgusted. But then the farmer gave them a taste of the blue milk, which they drank after some hesitation.

But after the first taste they licked their lips, they smacked their lips, they took one sip and a second sip, a mouthful, and then a long, long draught. And they smiled and grinned at each other, and they took each other by the hand, and – would you believe it? – they forgot all their everyday quarrels and worries, felt as happy as no king could ever be, and sang and danced, jigged and jazzed, jitterbugged and boogie-woogied as never before in all their lives!

Well, there is not much more to tell. The farmer gave up his farm and settled down in the village. He opened an inn which he called "The Blue Cow", where they sold only blue milk. But you only had to taste it once, and you never again wanted to drink anything else.

The village became a place marked with ten stars in the tourist guide book. People from all over the world came to see the blue cow and to sample the blue milk which made them forget their troubles, made them dance and be happy.

And the blue cow herself?

She gave milk, and more milk, and still more milk.
Clear, wonderful, blue milk, which never turned sour.

And the big strong handsome bull kept gazing dreamingly at his beloved blue cow, and she kept looking at her beloved big strong handsome bull.

They had their tails slung round each other's necks and were happy, very, very happy – happier even than all the blue-milk-drinking, dancing, singing, happy people who frequented the inn.

The March
to Death

DRAWINGS BY JOHN OLDAY
FIRST PUBLISHED IN 1943

This new edition (1995) of *The March to Death* consists of 41 anti-war political cartoons accompanied by contemporary press cuttings. It was first published by FREEDOM PRESS in 1943 and in spite of being in the middle of a fratricidal war, sold two editions – a total of 10,000 copies. Perhaps war in the European Union is now unthinkable but Chancellor Kohl of Germany recently suggested that if monetary union was not realised by 1999, the unthinkable could well become the reality. These Olday cartoons, and equally important, the quotes, confirm the anarchist contention that war is the health of capitalism.

FREEDOM PRESS   ISBN 0 900384 80 8   **£3.00**

These articles are a perceptive and prescient analysis of the politics and policies of the war and the following flowering of witch hunts of the west and the repressions of the east. Now we are away from the topicality of the dread dead disasters that spurred them see what now shines through: the author's warm humanism and intellectual honesty.

In the decades since we have gone from cold wars through detente to current glasnost. Bloody wars all the time. Marie-Louise stands firm for freedom, us against them. The choice before us all at every turn from entropy is expediency and comfort or the harder but more rewarding radical proposition that 'an injury to one is the concern of all' Read and marvel and work away at it.

£4.50

ISBN 0 900384 42 5

FREEDOM PRESS

Marie-Louise Berneri

NEITHER EAST NOR WEST

Selected Writings 1939-1948

INCLUDING

16 Anti-War Cartoons by John Olday

APPEARING **1943-1944** IN WAR COMMENTARY

FREEDOM PRESS